Volcanoes and Geysers

By Mary Draper

Contents

Introduction

Volcanoes and geysers are found in many parts of the world.

Some volcanoes often throw ash and lava into the air. Others have not erupted for a long time.

Whole cities and towns have been destroyed by the lava and ash that come out of volcanoes.

Many people live near volcanoes because the ash from volcanic eruptions is good for farming.

Geysers spurt hot water and steam into the air.

The water is heated deep underground.

How Volcanoes Are Made

Volcanoes usually happen at places where Earth's crust is cracked. The crust is the top layer of Earth, and is made of many giant pieces, called plates. The plates fit together like a jigsaw puzzle, but they are moving slowly all the time.

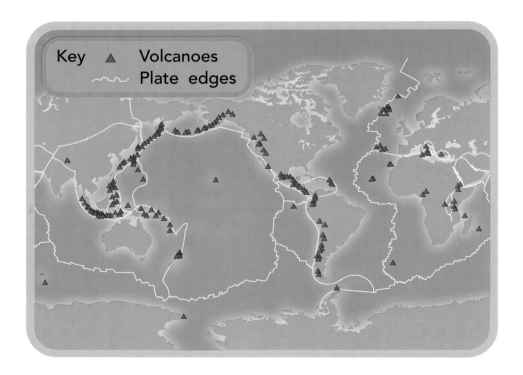

Just below the crust is a layer of hot rock. Sometimes the rock gets so hot that it melts and changes into a thick, boiling liquid called lava. The lava escapes through cracks in the crust. The cracks are usually near the edges of the plates. The lava cools and turns into hard rock. It builds up and forms a volcano.

DID YOU KNOW?

Scientists know where to find most volcanoes by learning about the movements of Earth's plates.

Active Volcanoes

Some volcanoes are active. This means that at any time they may throw out rocks, lava, and ash. When this happens, it is called an eruption.

Volcanoes erupt in different ways, and form different-shaped mountains.

Sometimes the lava flows out of the volcano like a river. People have time to move away to safety.

Other volcanoes give no warning that they are going to erupt. Mount St. Helens, in Washington, erupted suddenly in 1980. It spurted lava and ash high into the air, and some people could not escape from it.

DID YOU KNOW?

There are more than 500 active volcanoes in the world.

Mount St. Helens

Dormant Volcanoes

Dormant volcanoes do not erupt for a very long time. Sometimes they are dormant for hundreds of years. But they can suddenly wake up! Then they usually have strong eruptions.

Mount Pinatubo, in the Philippines, was a dormant volcano that suddenly woke up.

Mount Pinatubo

The Daily News, June 1991

Mount Pinatubo Erupts!

Mount Pinatubo had been dormant for 600 years, but yesterday it erupted suddenly. A huge cloud of ash is blocking the sunlight. Many people have had to leave their homes to escape from the ash and lava.

Sudden rain may cause mudslides, which can damage houses and roads. Many people will be homeless.

Vesuvius and the City of Pompeii

Nearly 2,000 years ago in Italy, Pompeii was a busy city. It lay at the foot of a dormant volcano, called Mount Vesuvius.

One summer's day, Mount Vesuvius suddenly erupted, and Pompeii was buried under hot, wet ash and mud.

About 200 years ago, people discovered this city and started to dig it up. The layer of ash had preserved many of the buildings and the things that people used in everyday life. Whole streets have been uncovered, and inside the homes are cooking pots and tools that were used 2,000 years ago.

cooking pots

DID YOU KNOW?

Mount Vesuvius is still active today. Scientists watch the volcano for signs of an eruption.

a street uncovered

Volcanoes Under the Ocean

Volcanoes can be found under the ocean. When they erupt, the water is so heavy that lava cannot flow easily. Sometimes the lava forms large lumps, called pillow lava.

Volcanoes that erupt under ocean waters can make islands. Ash, lava, and rock are tossed up into the sea. They slowly build an island. Later flows of lava help the island to grow.

Surtsey island was formed by volcanic eruptions. It took three years to form the island.

Surtsey Island

DID YOU KNOW?

The islands of Hawaii were made by volcanoes under the ocean.

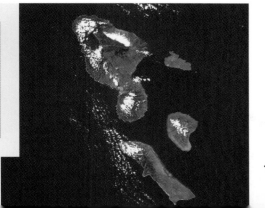

Volcanoes and People

Volcanoes are very dangerous, but they can help us, too.

The ash left by volcanic eruptions makes rich soil that is good for farming. Farmers sometimes grow their crops near the slopes of volcanoes.

Some volcanoes have a mineral called sulphur. Sulphur is used to make some medicines, and to make fertilizer, which helps plants grow.

People find volcanoes very interesting. We can visit famous volcanoes.

Geysers

Geysers are usually found near volcanoes. A geyser forms when water deep in Earth's crust heats up.

How a geyser forms

1. The hot water makes steam.

2. The steam escapes to Earth's surface through cracks.

3. The steam and hot water spurt into the air like a fountain.

Geysers can be exciting to watch.

Hot Pools

Sometimes hot water escapes from under the ground and lies in pools.

If the hot water has sulphur in it, it can smell really bad! The sulphur also makes rocks turn yellow.

DID YOU KNOW?

Hot water can turn volcanic ash
into hot mud.
Air bubbles push up through the mud
and make "plopping" noises.

21

Geysers and People

People from all over the world visit Yellowstone National Park. The park has more than 200 geysers. It also has hot pools and boiling mud pots.

People like to watch the geysers. But they need to stay back because the water is very hot.

People know that volcanoes and geysers can be very dangerous. But people have found ways to live with them.

Questions

1. How do scientists know where to find most volcanoes?
2. How many active volcanoes are there in the world?
3. Why do scientists watch Mount Vesuvius?
4. How were the islands of Hawaii made?
5. How is hot mud formed?
6. Why do some people bathe in mud from volcanoes and hot pools?

Glossary

active   awake; to be working or doing something

destroy   to tear down, break, or smash

dormant   asleep, not active

erupt   to blow up, burst out, or explode

mineral   something that is found in rock or soil

plates   the giant pieces that make up Earth's crust

preserve to keep something safe

Index

PM PLUS LEVELS

1
2
3
4
5
6
7
8
9
10
11
12
13
14
15
16
17
18
19
20
21
22
23

26
27
28
29
30

PM PLUS

NONFICTION LEVELS 24 & 25

ISBN 0 7578 1120 5

Incredible, Edible **PLANTS**

Benchmark EDUCATION

by Sarah Feldman

As you read …
think about the
different kinds of plants
you eat every day.

SCIENCE
Plants We Use

Level 20 K
Word Count: 531*

Incredible, Edible Plants
EARLY CONNECTIONS™

Benchmark Education Company
629 Fifth Avenue • Pelham, NY 10803

Credits:
Author: Sarah Feldman
Editor: Anne Flounders
Art Director: Jonette Jakobson
Photo Editor: Lynn Shen

Photo Credits: Page 2-3: Rob Lewine/CORBIS; Page 4: Gettyimages; Page 10B, 18, 19: Richard Warren

ISBN: 1-4108-1541-2

For ordering information call **Toll Free 1-877-236-2465** or visit our website at **www.benchmarkeducation.com.**

*The total word count for this book is based on words in black type and headings only. Words in photo captions, labels, diagrams, and charts appear in a different color (usually blue) and are not included. Numerals are not included.